Kids'
PARTY
Cakes

KÖNEMANN

Helpful Hints For Successful Cake Decorating

Cake making and decorating should be fun. Here are some hints to help make cake decorating enjoyable and successful without intricate designs or the use of a template.

◆ Assemble all the ingredients and utensils before you start baking or decorating the cake.
◆ Use the correct sized and shaped pans. We take our measurements across the top of pans.
◆ Prepare pans before you begin. Brush pan/s with melted butter or oil. Line base and sides with waxed or parchment paper; grease the paper.
◆ Preheat oven to moderate 350°F.
◆ Establish size of board to be used, allowing ample space around the cake. Masonite is ideal for a cake board.
◆ Boards can be covered with foil, foil-covered paper, cellophane or wrapping paper of your choice.

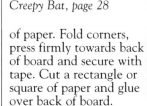

Creepy Bat, page 28

◆ To cover a round board, cut a circle 2 inches larger than the board. Spread smooth surface of board with children's glue and press into center of wrong side of paper. Cut extension at 1-inch intervals around board. Fold paper over edge of board and secure to back of board with tape. Cut out a paper circle and glue over back of board.
◆ To cover a rectangular or square board, cut paper 2 inches larger than the board. Spread smooth surface of board with children's glue and press into center of wrong side of paper. Fold corners, press firmly towards back of board and secure with tape. Cut a rectangle or square of paper and glue over back of board.
◆ Bake cakes for suggested time or until a wooden skewer or toothpick inserted near the center comes out clean. (Cakes baked in oven-proof bowls take longer, about 50 minutes.)

Basic Butter Cake
¼ cup butter
1 cup sugar
1 egg, lightly beaten
1 teaspoon vanilla
1¼ cups all-purpose flour
1½ teaspoons baking powder
⅔ cup milk

WARNING Always remove skewers from cakes before you serve them. Never use toothpicks to hold cakes together. They can easily be hidden in a serving and a child can choke on them.

1 Preheat oven to moderate 350°F. Brush pan (see chart, opposite, for sizes) with melted butter or oil. Line base and sides with waxed or parchment paper; grease paper.
2 Using electric beaters, beat butter and sugar in small mixing bowl until light and creamy. Add egg and beat thoroughly. Add vanilla; beat until combined.
3 Stir together flour and baking powder. Using a metal spoon, fold in flour mixture alternately with milk. Stir until just combined and mixture is almost smooth. Be careful not to overmix.
4 Spoon mixture into prepared pan; smooth surface. Bake 35 minutes or until a skewer comes out clean when it is inserted in center of cake.
5 Leave cake in pan 10 minutes before turning onto wire rack to cool. Remove paper.

Butter cakes can be baked up to 3 months before using. Cover with plastic wrap and store in freezer. Remove from freezer, stand, uncovered, 10 minutes before cutting to shape. Stand further 15 minutes before decorating. Freeze leftover cake pieces and use later for desserts, if desired.

Fluffy Icing
1 cup sugar
⅓ cup water
2 egg whites

1 Combine sugar and water in small pan. Stir constantly over low heat until mixture boils and sugar has dissolved. Simmer, uncovered, without stirring for 5 minutes.
2 Using electric beaters, beat egg whites in a clean, dry mixing bowl until stiff peaks form.
3 Pour hot syrup in a thin stream over egg whites, beating constantly until icing is thick, glossy and increased in volume.

Basic Butter Cream
⅓ cup butter
4 cups powdered sugar, sifted
¼ cup milk
1 teaspoon vanilla

1 Beat butter in small mixing bowl until light and creamy.
2 Gradually add 2 cups sugar, beating well. Add milk and vanilla, beating well. Add remaining sugar and beat till well combined.

You will need 1 package 1-layer size cake mix or 1 quantity Basic Butter Cake to fill the following sized pans.	
8 x 1½-inch or 9 x 1½-inch	round cake pan
8 x 8 x 2-inch	square cake pan
8-inch	tube pan
11 x 7 x 1½-inch	shallow oblong cake pan
9 x 5 x 2-inch	bread/loaf pan
5-cup capacity	oven-proof bowl
12	cupcakes

You will need 1 package 2-layer size cake mix or 2 quantities Basic Butter Cake to fill the following sized pans.	
2 8 x 1½-inch or 9 x 1½-inch	round cake pans
2 8 x 8 x 2-inch	square cake pans
13 x 9 x 2-inch	rectangular cake pan
15 x 10 x 1-inch	jelly roll pan
7-cup capacity	oven-proof bowl
9-cup capacity	oven-proof bowl
10-cup capacity	oven-proof bowl
24	cupcakes

Drum

1 covered board
2 8- or 9-inch round
   Basic Butter Cakes or
   purchased sponge cakes
⅓ cup strawberry jam
1 quantity Basic Butter
   Cream
green food coloring
1 yard green ribbon
licorice or fruit-flavored
   candy squares
2 chopsticks
candy for drum sticks
colored dragees

1 Sandwich cakes
together with jam.
Position on board.
2 Tint half the butter
cream pale green. Divide
remaining butter cream
into two portions. Leave
one portion plain, tint
second portion dark
green. Spread plain icing
over top of drum; pale
green icing around side
of drum.

3 Cut ribbon into
required lengths to fit
around side of drum.
Press ribbon onto side of
cake in zig-zag pattern.
4 Press licorice or fruit-
flavored candy onto side
of cake. Pipe dark green
icing over top rim of
drum. Cover chopsticks
with foil and place
candy on ends to make
drumsticks. Complete
cake, as illustrated.

HINT
Colored dragees
(small decorative
balls) add a festive
look to decorated
cakes, but be sure to
read the label.
Some dragees are not
edible and should
be removed from
the cake before
serving.

1. Spread strawberry jam over cake and
place second cake on top.

2. Spread plain icing over the top of drum
and pale green icing around sides.

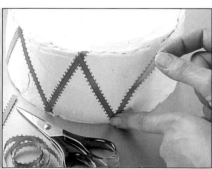

3. Cut green ribbon and arrange in a zig-zag pattern around drum.

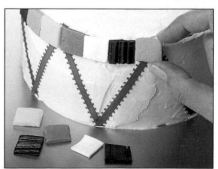

4. Arrange licorice or fruit-flavored candy around sides of drum.

Teddy Bear

1 Basic Butter Cake from
  9-cup oven-proof bowl
1 Basic Butter Cake from
  5-cup oven-proof bowl
1 purchased 6½ x 3-inch
  pound cake, angel food
  cake or banana bread
1 quantity Fluffy Icing
red and yellow food coloring
2 round flat chocolate-
  covered cookies
licorice strips
2 plastic eyes
assorted candy
14 inches of ribbon

1 Cut 1 inch off one
end of large cake and
½ inch off opposite end.
Stand on prepared board
on 1 inch cut edge.
2 Cut ½ inch off one
end of smaller cake.
Attach head to body
with skewers. Cut pound
cake crosswise into 4
even portions. Set aside
2 of the portions for the
legs. Trim to size. Halve
1 of the remaining
portions lengthwise for
arms. Attach pound cake
portions onto cake with
skewers. Tint all but 1
cup icing with 1 drop red
and 3 drops yellow food
coloring to make brown.
3 Spread tinted icing
over all of cake. Attach
cookies to head with
skewers.
4 Decorate cake, as
illustrated.

1. Cut a slice off both ends
of large bowl cake.

2. Assemble cake with
skewers.

3. Swirl plain icing onto
belly, head and paws.

4. Decorate cake with eyes,
cookies, candy, and bow.

HINT

We've chosen to make this cake in the
traditional teddy bear color of brown. But he
could just as easily be covered with blue, red or
green icing, or stripes or polka dots. There's no
reason for teddy to be a male, either. A girl teddy
could be iced in pink, adorned with a bright pink
bow, and given some yellow popcorn for her hair.
Cake decorating is a form of self-expression—so
express yourself!

Happy Humpty on the Wall

1 covered board
1 8- or 9-inch round
  Basic Butter Cake or
  purchased sponge cake
1 13 x 9 x 2-inch Basic
  Butter Cake
2 quantities Basic Butter
  Cream
yellow food coloring
rectangular chocolate-
  covered cookies
assorted candy
20 inches colored ribbon

1 Using a sharp knife, trim the edges of round cake to form an egg shape.
2 Position cut Humpty shape onto rectangular cake (wall), using skewers. Tint Basic Butter Cream yellow.
3 Spread front, back, top and sides of the wall smoothly with two-thirds of the tinted icing. Press the chocolate cookies onto wall in a brick pattern as shown, cutting them to fit. Spread remaining icing all over Humpty's head.
4 Decorate Humpty's face with assorted candy, as illustrated. Position a big ribbon bow onto Humpty's neck last.

1. Cut round cake into oval shape for Humpty.

2. Attach two cakes with skewers.

3. Press chocolate cookies into wall in brick pattern.

4. Make face with candy and finish with bow.

HINT
This is one of the easiest cakes to make, ideal for a first-time cake decorator. Children can help with the decorating, too, for their own party or for a younger brother or sister.
Make sure the Basic Butter Cream is at room temperature before you ice the cake. If it is too cold, it will be hard to spread, and rough handling could cause the cake to crumble into pieces.

Clown

1 covered board
1 9-inch round Basic
  Butter Cake
1 Basic Butter Cake from
  5-cup oven-proof bowl
2 quantities Basic Butter
  Cream
pink, black, blue, yellow,
  violet and green food
  coloring
3 purchased miniature
  cream-filled cake rolls
1 large muffin
2 plastic eyes
licorice twists
toasted or white
  marshmallow
assorted candy

1 Place round cake
onto prepared board.
Turn bowl cake on its
side; cut ½ inch off one
end of cake. Attach,
cut-side down, onto
round cake with skewers.
2 Cut ½-inch slice
diagonally off one side of
head; hat will be placed
here. Divide icing into
three portions. Tint all
but 1 tablespoon of one
portion deep pink; tint
remaining tablespoon
dark grey. Tint two-
thirds of second portion
pale pink; make
remaining one-third
blue. Divide third
portion of icing into
three portions; tint
yellow, violet and green.
Spread base, with two-

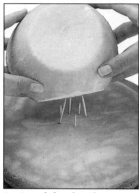

1. Attach head with
skewers.

2. Ice top and sides of
miniature cake rolls.

3. Pipe smiling mouth on
clown in deep pink icing.

4. Place muffin in position
for hat; decorate face.

thirds deep pink icing;
spread pale pink over
head. Cover top and
sides of miniature cake
rolls with desired
colored icings. Cut in
half crosswise and
arrange on cake with cut
side toward head.
3 Pipe mouth onto cake
with reserved deep pink

and overpipe a smiling
line in dark grey or use
licorice strips.
4 Cut off rounded top
of muffin (hat) and
spread with blue icing;
attach hat to side of
head with skewers or
icing. Position eyes onto
face. To complete cake,
decorate as shown.

10

Alphabet Blocks

1 covered board
2 8-inch square Basic
 Butter Cakes
1 quantity Basic Butter
 Cream
pink, yellow, green,
 apricot and violet food
 coloring
miniature colored
 marshmallows

1 Sandwich both cakes together with some of the butter cream. Trim edges; cut cake into four squares.
2 Divide icing into six portions. Tint two portions pink and each of the four remaining portions a different color. Spread a different color icing over each side of blocks.
3 Pipe a shell border along edge of each side of the blocks with one portion of pink icing.

4 Carefully arrange onto prepared board, as shown. Decorate with marshmallows, as shown.

HINT
These blocks may be decorated any way that appeals to you. You can pipe faces onto them, or people, objects or animals; you can make abstract designs with icing or candy; you can put numbers on them; or your children can make up their own patterns. It's important to arrange the blocks before you do your final decorations, because if they're moved, you could ruin your design.

1. Sandwich cakes with butter cream and cut into four squares.

2. Spread a different-colored icing on each side of blocks.

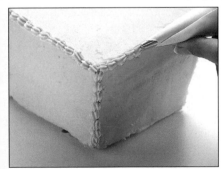

3. Pipe a shell border in pink icing around all the edges.

4. Arrange cakes on board and decorate with miniature colored marshmallows.

1. Spread sandwiched cakes with icing and cover with sprinkles.

2. Pipe lines to indicate frills and fill in with colored icing.

14

Jack-in-the-Box

1 covered board
2 8-inch square Basic
  Butter Cakes
2 8-inch round Basic
  Butter Cakes or
  purchased sponge cakes
2 quantities Basic Butter
  Cream
colored sprinkles
blue, violet, orange,
  yellow and red food
  coloring
licorice strips
assorted candy
marshmallows

1 Sandwich square cakes together with some of the butter cream. Place on prepared board. Divide icing into two portions. Spread one portion plain icing over square cake; reserve ⅔ cup for face. Press sprinkles over top and sides of square cake with a small metal spatula.

2 Divide remaining icing into four portions. Tint each one a different color (not including red). Pipe lines with plain icing onto one round cake to mark frills. Spread colors alternately onto cake within the lines, as shown.

3 Position iced round cake onto sprinkle-covered cake. Cut licorice into pieces. Arrange on iced round cake, as shown, with marshmallows.

4 Position head (remaining round cake) onto decorated round cake using skewers. Tint reserved plain icing yellow. Spread over head. Tint 2 teaspoons leftover yellow icing red for the lips. Pipe lips onto face, as shown. Complete cake, as illustrated.

3. Arrange licorice strips and marshmallows on round cake.

4. Place Jack's head on round cake and ice and decorate, as shown.

15

Numbers 1-10.

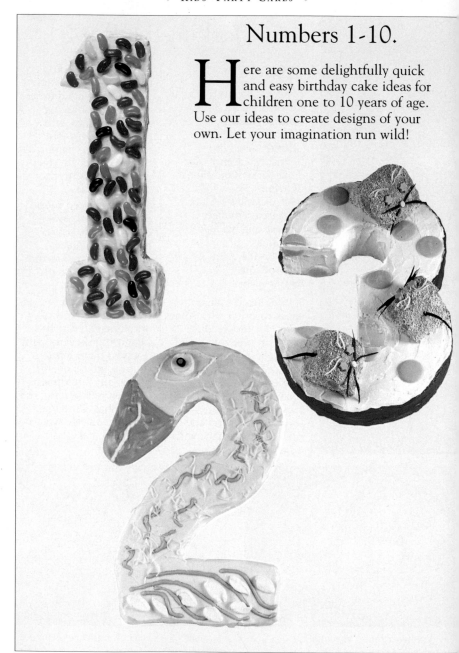

Here are some delightfully quick and easy birthday cake ideas for children one to 10 years of age. Use our ideas to create designs of your own. Let your imagination run wild!

1 covered board
1 8-inch square Basic
   Butter Cake
1 quantity Basic Butter
   Cream
yellow food coloring
jelly beans

1 Cut cake into 3 equal strips. Leave one strip of cake as is (1).
2 Cut 2 inches off the end of the second strip of cake (2).
3 Cut remaining strip of cake in half. Cut diagonally across one of these portions for the top of the number (3).
4 Tint butter cream yellow, assemble and decorate cake, as shown.

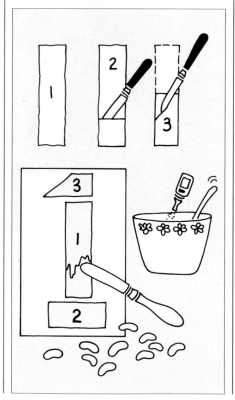

1 covered board
1 8-inch square Basic
   Butter Cake
1 8-inch round Basic
   Butter Cake
1 quantity Fluffy Icing
pink food coloring
candy for eye
6 marshmallows

1 Cut a portion off square cake to measure 8 x 2½ inches. Cut about 2 inches off this piece. Use long piece for base of number two. Reserve small piece.
2 Cut a 2-inch circle out of the center of round cake to make a ring cake. Reserve center. Cut out ⅕ of the ring cake. Assemble cake pieces on board, as shown. For beak, cut out a piece of cake from reserved center.
3 Tint ⅔ cup icing dark pink, all but 2 tablespoons pale pink.
4 Decorate cake, as illustrated.

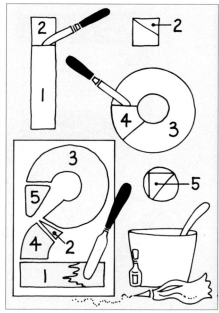

1 covered board
2 8-inch round Basic
  Butter Cakes
1 quantity Basic
  Butter Cream
red and black
  food coloring
assorted candy
licorice strips
flaked and shredded coconut

1 Cut a 2-inch circle out of center of cakes. Cut out ¼ of first ring cake; place remainder on board as base of number. Cut out ⅓ of second cake; shape to fit against base.
2 Cut three half circles from leftover cake pieces for mice.
3 Divide icing in two. Leave one portion plain. Tint all but ½ cup of remaining icing red; tint remaining icing grey.
4 Decorate, as illustrated.

1 covered board
1 13 x 9 x 2-inch
  Basic Butter Cake
1 quantity Fluffy Icing
blue food coloring
silver dragees
tiny posy of flowers
ribbon

1 Cut cake into 3 13-inch strips. Place one strip of cake onto board. Cut one-quarter off second strip of cake, set aside. Cut diagonally across each end of remaining strip of cake.
2 Assemble cake, as shown.
3 Tint icing light blue. Spread over top and sides of cake.
4 Decorate, as illustrated.

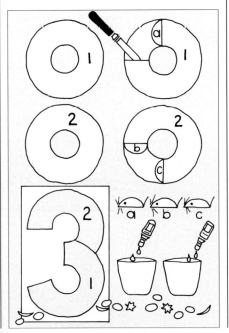

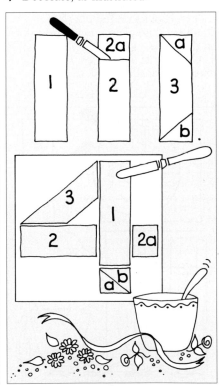

19

1 covered board
1 13 x 9 x 2-inch
   Basic Butter
   Cake
1 quantity Basic
   Butter Cream
yellow food coloring
10–12 rectangular
   chocolate-covered
   cookies
licorice strips

1 Cut one 8-inch ring out of cake.
Cut remaining cake into one strip
measuring 8 x 2½ inches. Cut about ⅓
off this strip. Cut out ¼ of ring cake.
Assemble cake on board, as shown.
2 Reserve 2 tablespoons plain icing.
Tint remaining icing yellow.
3 Cover cake with yellow icing. Press
enough cookies on top of cake for
dominoes. Use plain icing to pipe dots
on dominoes.
4 Cut licorice into strips. Position
onto cake, as illustrated.

1 covered board
1 13 x 9 x 2-inch
   Basic Butter Cake
1 quantity Basic
   Butter Cream
twisted licorice cut
   into ½-inch pieces
assorted candy for
   face
green and violet food coloring

1 Cut one 8-inch ring out of cake.
Cut remaining cake into one strip
measuring 8 x 2½ inches. Cut strip of
cake ¾ inch diagonally across one end
and 1½ inches diagonally across the
other. The larger end will be used for
the top of the number.
2 Assemble cake, as shown.
3 Tint all but ½ cup icing bright green.
Tint 2 teaspoons icing violet, and
remaining icing pale green.
4 Spread top and sides of cake with
bright green icing. Use pale green for
scales; violet for brows. Decorate cake,
as illustrated.

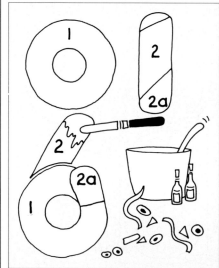

1 covered board
1 8-inch square Basic
 Butter Cake
1 quantity Basic
 Butter Cream
caramel and orange
 food coloring
licorice strip
assorted candy

1 Cut cake into two 8 x 2½-inch strips. Place one strip of cake onto board for top of number seven and cut a small curve into top left side. Round off end for nose and cut another shallow curve on right side of cake.
2 Cut second strip of cake ½ inch diagonally across both ends. Position one of cut-out pieces on top of second cake, as shown. Assemble cakes.
3 Tint all but 1 cup icing caramel-brown; spread over cake. Tint reserved icing orange. Pipe blotches, as shown. Tint leftover icing dark orange. Use to outline blotches.
4 Cut licorice into pieces for mane. Decorate, as illustrated.

1 covered board
2 8-inch round Basic
 Butter Cakes
1 quantity Basic
 Butter Cream
blue food coloring
licorice strips
1 plastic train set

1 Cut a 2-inch circle out of the center of each cake. Cut ¾ inch off base of both and assemble, as shown.
2 Tint icing blue; spread over top and sides of cake.
3 Cut licorice into long strips and short strips. Position long strips on cake for railway line. Place short strips across tracks.
4 Complete cake, as shown.

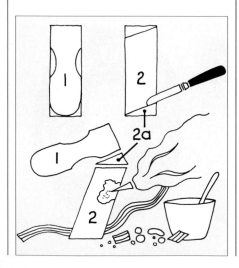

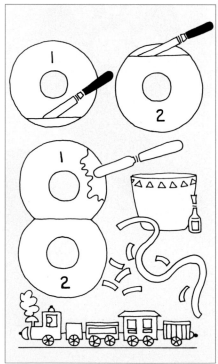

1 covered board
1 13 x 9 x 2-inch
  Basic Butter Cake
1 quantity Basic
  Butter Cream
blue and orange
  food coloring
leaf-shaped candy
marshmallows
yellow sprinkles
assorted candy

1 Cut one 8-inch ring out of cake. Cut remaining cake into an 8 x 2½-inch strip. Place ring cake onto board. Cut 1½ inches diagonally across one end of strip of cake. Curve slightly to fit against ring cake. Tint ½ cup icing orange; remaining icing blue.
2 Spread top and sides of cake with blue icing.
3 Pipe orange petals onto cake, fill with orange icing, as shown.
4 Cut marshmallows in half. Pinch ends to shape. Top with sprinkles. Complete cake, as illustrated.

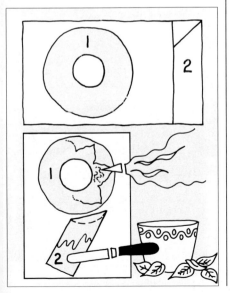

2 cupcakes
2 quantities Basic
  Butter Cream
red and black food
  coloring
10 flat white mints
  or candy
silver dragees
20 inches red
  curling ribbon
1 covered board

1 13 x 9 x 2-inch
Basic Butter Cake

1 Cut one 8-inch ring out of cake. Cut remaining cake into two 8 x 2-inch strips. Place one strip of cake on its side, on board. Place a cupcake at each end as earpiece and mouthpiece for receiver. Cut second strip of cake in half. Reserve half for another use.
2 Cut remaining half in two. Cut ring cake in half. Assemble cakes on board, as shown.
3 Tint all but 3 tablespoons icing red. Tint remaining icing black. Spread top and sides of cakes with red icing.
4 Pipe black numbers onto mints. Decorate cakes, as illustrated.

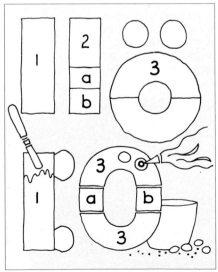

Pirate Pete

1 covered board
1 13 x 9 x 2-inch Basic
  Butter Cake
2 quantities Basic Butter
  Cream
violet, caramel and
  chocolate-brown food
  coloring
1 8-inch round Basic
  Butter Cake or
  purchased sponge cake
20 toothpicks
flat round chocolate-
  covered cookie
assorted candy
licorice strip

1 Cut rectangular cake
into shape of hat, as
shown.
2 Position hat on
board. Reserve ⅓ cup
plain icing. Divide
remaining icing into
three portions. Tint one
portion dark violet,
second portion caramel
and third portion

chocolate-brown. Spread
violet over hat.
3 Position head (round
cake) onto hat. Spread
caramel icing over head.
Use brown icing to pipe
pirate's hair.
4 Tape toothpicks
together firmly. Dip ends
into brown food coloring
and dab onto pirate's
chin, as shown. Pipe
skull and crossbones and
right eye with plain
icing in small bag. Cut a
small piece diagonally
off cookie for eye patch.
Complete cake, as
illustrated.

HINT

Add food coloring to
icing gradually. Use
the tip of a skewer to
tint small amounts of
icing; an eye dropper
can be used for larger
quantities.

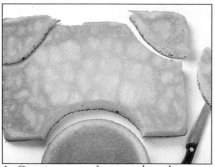

1. Cut pieces out of rectangular cake to
form hat shape.

2. Place hat on prepared board and cover
with violet icing.

3. Position head on board, ice and pipe on brown icing for hair.

4. Decorate face. Use toothpicks dipped in brown food coloring to dab on whiskers.

Miss Dolly

1 covered board
1 Basic Butter Cake from
    10-cup oven-proof bowl
1 quantity Basic Butter
    Cream
6-inch hard plastic doll
red and yellow food
    coloring
12 pink ribbon roses
silver and pink dragees
16 inches of lace
    trimming

1 Trim cake surface.
Center cake on prepared
board and attach with a
little icing. Press doll
firmly but carefully into
cake to waist level. Tint
one-third icing yellow.
Tint ⅓ cup icing light
pink; tint remaining
icing dark red.
2 Mark underskirt
scallops onto cake with a
skewer. Pipe yellow icing
in rows onto cake,
starting at base of
underskirt.
3 Swirl dark red icing
onto remaining cake.
Pipe dark red icing on
bodice and light pink
trim on dress.
4 Decorate cake, as
shown. Position lace
onto dress last.

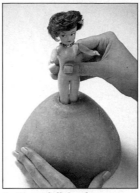

1. Press doll firmly into
cake up to waist.

2. Pipe underskirt scallops
onto base.

3. Swirl red icing onto
remaining cake.

4. Place lace around bottom
of dress last.

HINT

To make a disposable piping bag, you will need a
sheet of parchment or waxed paper 12 x 12
inches or 12 x 16 inches. Fold in half lengthwise.
Fold and twist paper to form a cone. Tape or
staple along outside of cone. For a shortcut
version that doesn't require a nozzle, use a heavy
plastic sandwich bag or envelope. Half fill bag
with icing, seal and snip the point off one of the
corners.

Creepy Bat

1 covered board
1 9-inch round Basic
   Butter Cake
2-inch round cutter
1 quantity Fluffy Icing
black food coloring
assorted candy

1 Cut cake in half. For
bat wings, cut three half
circles along straight
edge of each cake half
using the cutter to form
scallops.
2 Arrange the bat
wings onto prepared
board. Join 2 half circles
together for bat body as
shown. Tint all but 1
cup icing dark grey. Tint
remaining icing black.
Spread grey icing over
top of wings and bat
body. Give the icing on
the wings a rough
texture with a fork.
Spread all but 2

tablespoons black icing
below wings.
3 Pipe black icing
around body and wings
as shown.
4 Insert skewers into
candy for ears and attach
to head. Decorate cake,
as illustrated. Stick-on
stars and moons may be
placed on the board, if
desired.

HINT
Trim top and sides of
cakes with a serrated
knife for best results.
Use underside of
cake as top; it will
produce a smoother,
flatter surface.
Fully-iced cakes can
be made ahead and
frozen for up to
three months.
Decorate with candy
and ribbons, etc,
on the day to be
used.

1. Using cutter, cut three half circles from straight edge of each cake half.

2. Place pieces on board, cover top of wings and body with dark grey icing.

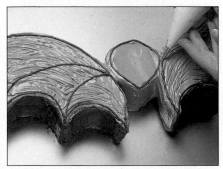

3. Pipe black icing to outline bat body and wings.

4. Decorate face, as shown. Use skewers to attach candy as ears.

Robby Robot

1 covered board
1 9 x 5 x 2-inch Basic
   Butter Cake loaf
1 purchased 6½ x 3-inch
   pound cake or other cake
1 quantity Basic Butter
   Cream
red, green, orange and
   violet food coloring
4 lollipops
2 chocolate-covered candy
   sticks or cookies
assorted candy

1 Stand loaf cake upright on prepared board, with top of loaf facing the front. Trim base, if necessary. Cut pound cake in half crosswise. Using one of the halves, cut it into 2 rounded feet for the robot. Position feet at base of robot, as shown.
2 Trim remaining half of pound cake down to a 3-inch circle for head. Divide icing into two portions. Tint one portion red. Leave ½ cup untinted. Tint 3 tablespoons green, 1 tablespoon orange and remaining icing violet. Spread red icing on body and violet on feet. Make a rectangle in center of body with plain icing for control panel. Spread head with plain icing; attach it to the body with skewers or icing.

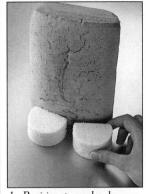

1. Position pound cake pieces at base for feet.

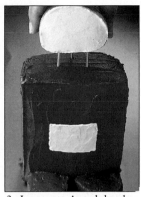

2. Ice parts. Attach head to body with skewers.

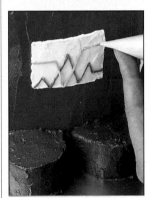

3. Pipe details on body.

4. Press lollipops into sides for arms.

3 Pipe orange lines and mouth. Pipe green lines, dots on feet and squiggles around face.
4 Press lollipops into sides of cake for arms; attach candy sticks to head for antennae. Decorate remaining cake, as illustrated.

HINT
Spread a small quantity of icing onto the prepared board and place cake on it. This will prevent the cake from sliding around when it is being decorated, transported or stored.

Spinning Spaceship

1 covered board
1 8- or 9-inch round Basic
  Butter Cake
1 quantity Fluffy Icing
red, black and yellow food
  coloring
licorice strips
2 chocolate-covered
  marshmallow cookies
silver dragees
4 lollipops
assorted candy

1   Cut a 3-inch wide
slice across the cake and
cut this slice in
half.
2   Place halves onto
prepared board, on
either side of the
remaining cake (which
is the ship body), as
shown.
3   Tint ¼ cup icing red
and ¼ cup icing black.
Reserve 1 tablespoon

plain icing. Tint
remaining icing yellow.
Spread the yellow icing
over the main body of
the spaceship and over
the base.
4   Use red and black
icings to pipe windows
and lines, as shown.
Place licorice onto
spaceship, as shown.
Position marshmallow
cookies and lollipops, as
shown. Pipe on face
with plain icing.
Complete decorating
cake, as shown.

HINT
Use piping bags with
or without nozzles for
the finishing touches.
Use a paper piping
bag and discard when
finished or use a cloth
or plastic bag.

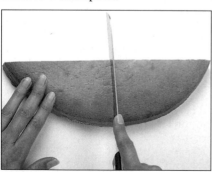

1. Cut a slice off bottom of cake, and cut it in half.

2. Position pieces on either side of remaining cake.

3. Frost top and base of spaceship with yellow icing.

4. Pipe on details; position cookies, candy and lollipops.

Sam Snowman

1 covered board
5-inch cardboard circle
1 Basic Butter Cake from
   9-cup oven-proof bowl
1 Basic Butter Cake from
   5-cup oven-proof bowl
1 quantity Fluffy Icing
black food coloring
1 large purchased cupcake
   or muffin
colored dragees
assorted candy
twisted licorice stick
20 inches ribbon
toothpicks
rubber band

1. Cut out ring from cardboard circle.

2. Cover head and body with plain icing.

1 Cut a 1½-inch circle from center of 5-inch cardboard circle to form a ring. Place large cake onto prepared board. Stand small cake on its side, cut ¾ inch across cake. Position small cake on larger cake using skewers or icing to attach.
2 Tint 1 cup icing black; leave remaining icing plain. Spread plain icing roughly over snowman.
3 Spread black icing onto one side of cardboard ring and muffin. Position ring onto snowman's head. Attach muffin to cake with skewers through center of ring to make hat.

3. For hat, place muffin on ring and ice black.

4 Decorate hat with dragees and add finishing touches, as shown. Place ribbon around snowman's neck and tie loosely. Do this last. To make broom, attach toothpicks to licorice stick with rubber band.

4. Make broom out of toothpicks and licorice.

HINT
Flat-bladed knives, small metal spatulas, rubber or plastic spatulas are ideal for spreading icing onto cakes. Forks can be used for swirling or creating lines or special effects on the icing.

1. Trim sides off strip of cake for peaked roof; place on top of trimmed oval cake.

2. Frost ark and roof, as shown.

Noah's Ark

1 covered board
1 13 x 9 x 2-inch Basic
  Butter Cake
2 quantities Basic Butter
  Cream
orange, pink and violet
  food coloring
waffle cookies
assorted candy
small plastic animals

1 Cut 1½ inches off each long side of the cake to make 2 strips. Cut strips into two 7-inch lengths. Cut corners off remaining cake to form a long narrow oval. Place on prepared board.
2 Divide icing into three portions. Tint one orange, one pink and one violet. Place long cut sides of 7-inch strips together and glue together with violet icing to form cabin. Trim to

form a peaked roof. Set aside. Spread orange over sides of ark. Spread pink on deck. Place cabin on deck and frost with violet icing, as shown.
3 Press halved waffle cookies onto both sides of the cabin roof.
4 Arrange cookies or candy around the base of the ark. Place round candy on sides of cabin for windows. Complete cake, as shown.

HINT
The basic food colors of red, yellow, green, and blue can be found at most grocery stores. Otherwise try specialty food stores.

3. Stick waffle cookies on both sides of shaped roof.

4. Cover sides with licorice or candy logs; decorate with animals and candy.

Wilma Witch

1 covered board
1 13 x 9 x 2-inch Basic
  Butter Cake
1 8-inch square Basic
  Butter Cake
1 quantity Fluffy Icing
orange, violet, green and
  blue food coloring
currants and raisin
licorice twists and strips
assorted candy

1 Cut out hat from
rectangular cake and
witch head from square
cake, as shown.
2 Arrange cakes on
prepared board. Tint half
icing orange, 3
tablespoons icing violet
for lips, 1 tablespoon
green for veins in eye,
remaining icing blue for
hat.
3 Using a small metal
spatula, spread blue icing
over hat; orange over
face.
4 Pipe lips onto cake.
Using appropriate candy,
place teeth and eye onto
cake; pipe veins on eye.
Use currants for warts
on chin and raisin for
mole on nose. Arrange
licorice for hair, and
make insects on hat out
of candy. Decorate with
remaining candy, as
illustrated.

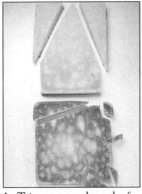

1. Trim rectangular cake for
hat, square cake for head.

2. Place cakes in position
on board.

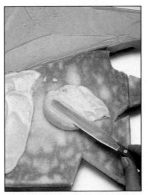

3. Use blue icing for hat,
orange for face.

4. Pipe lips. Add eye, teeth
and hair. Decorate.

HINT

Piping nozzles help add a professional look to
home-decorated cakes. The nozzles come in
different sizes and are available at department
stores, kitchenware shops and specialty cake
decorating shops. To use a nozzle, cut ¼ inch off
the end of bag before filling it with icing. Insert
nozzle, then spoon icing into bag; press towards
tip. Fold ends over bag to enclose icing. Use a
slow and steady squeeze to pipe icing onto cake.

Lovable Lucy

1 covered board
1 8- or 9-inch round Basic
   Butter Cake or
   purchased sponge cake
1 13 x 9 x 2-inch Basic
   Butter Cake
2 cupcakes or muffins
2 quantities Basic Butter
   Cream
pink and green food coloring
2 cups colored popcorn
2 toasted or white
   marshmallows
assorted candy
pink dragees
plastic eyes
8 inches lace trim
2 bows

1 Place round cake at top of prepared board. Shape rectangular cake into dress, as shown. Position onto board with head. Add cupcakes for feet. Cut cake trimmings down to size for arms and position onto board.
2 Reserve ½ cup plain icing for feet. Tint 1 cup icing pink for skin; tint remaining icing green for dress. Spread pink over face and arms, green over dress and plain icing over feet.
3 Press popcorn onto head for hair. Use marshmallows at ends of arms for hands.
4 Decorate cake as shown.

1. Cut oblong cake to shape; assemble all pieces.

2. Spread colored icings over head and body.

3. Use colored popcorn on round cake for hair.

4. Decorate feet with ribbon bows.

Hint
Always place cake into position on your prepared board before you start to decorate. If you decorate a cake, then try to move it, you can undo all your good work. If you're worried about drips as you go, choose foil or foil-covered paper to cover the board—spills can easily be wiped off. In hot weather, refrigerate an iced cake if it has to stand for any length of time before the party, otherwise chocolates and candy may melt.

Cool Cat

1 covered board
1 8- or 9-inch round Basic
   Butter Cake
1 quantity Fluffy Icing
pink, caramel and black
   food coloring
licorice strips
2 large white
   marshmallows
2 small round black
   candies

1 Cut cake into cat face
shape, as shown. Place
cake in position on
prepared board.
2 Tint 2 tablespoons
icing pale pink, 2
tablespoons black and ½
cup icing dark caramel.
Tint all but 2
tablespoons of the
remaining icing pale
caramel. Mark cat's facial
features onto the cake
with a skewer and pipe
features onto cake with
the plain icing. Fill in
mouth with pink icing.
3 Spread muzzle with
dark caramel icing, nose
with black. Spread pale
caramel icing over
remainder of cake. Make
pink triangles in ears.
4 Outline muzzle and
features with black, as
shown. Cut licorice
strips and use for
eyebrows and whiskers;
use black candy for
pupils of marshmallow
eyes. Complete cake, as
illustrated.

> ### Hint
> Let your children
> help decorate the
> cake if they wish.
> The cake may not
> be as professional as
> you would like, but
> your children will
> love it and be
> proud of their
> contribution.

1. Cut cake into cat shape, as shown, and
place on board.

2. Mark out facial features and pipe with
plain icing. Fill mouth with pink icing.

3. Ice muzzle with dark caramel, nose with black, rest of face with pale caramel.

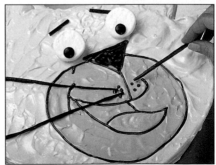

4. Outline face with black, and decorate with licorice strips and candy.

Perfect Parfait

1 covered board
1 13 x 9 x 2-inch Basic
  Butter Cake
4 purchased cupcakes
1 quantity Fluffy Icing
yellow, violet, caramel and
  pink food coloring
colored sprinkles
assorted candy

1 Cut the rectangular cake into the shape of a tall parfait glass, and place it onto the prepared board. Position the cupcakes at the top of the glass, as shown, cutting one of them into pieces to make the top look more like realistic scoops of ice cream.
2 Leave 1 cup icing plain. Tint ⅓ cup icing violet, ⅓ pink, ¼ cup caramel and remainder yellow. Spread caramel over base of glass.
3 Spread colored icings onto cake, as shown. Swirl plain icing over cupcakes.
4 Decorate cupcakes with colored sprinkles. Decorate the body of the glass with candy, as illustrated. We've chosen candy in the same colors as the icings, but you can use contrasting colors, if you prefer.

1. Cut cake into glass shape; top with cupcakes.

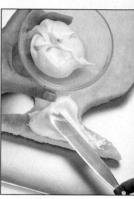

2. Spread base of parfait glass with caramel icing.

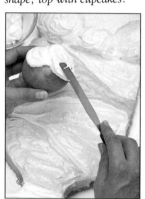

3. Ice rest of glass and cupcakes, as shown.

4. Finish with candy and sprinkles.

HINT

Place flaked or shredded coconut into a sealable plastic bag with 1 drop food coloring. Close bag and rub color into coconut with fingertips to desired shade, adding more color, if necessary. You can get a very interesting effect by using multi-colored coconut on iced cakes. To toast coconut, spread on a baking sheet and bake at 350°F about 5 minutes or until golden, stirring regularly.

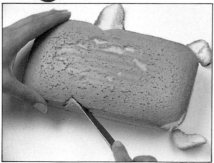

1. Cut into sides and curve end of loaf cake
to shape dog's body.

2. Place muffins and cake pieces into place
to form the parts of the dog's body.

Rusty the Dog

1 covered board
1 9 x 5 x 2-inch Basic
    Butter Cake loaf
2 large muffins
1 8-inch square Basic
    Butter Cake
2 quantities Basic Butter
    Cream
yellow food coloring
¼ cup unsweetened cocoa
    powder, sifted
1 teaspoon shredded
    coconut
assorted candy

1 Place loaf cake onto a cutting board, right side up. Round ends of cake. Cut curves into sides of cake for body.
2 Position on prepared board. Trim muffin for head to fit against body, as shown. Cut rounded tops off remaining muffin and cut in half vertically to form 2 half-circles. Cut a portion of the square cake into four 1 x 4-inch rectangles. Attach a muffin half to either side of cake for hind legs. Position small cake rectangles onto board for front legs and paws of hind legs. Cut remaining cake to form ears and tail. Assemble, as shown.
3 Tint ¾ icing yellow. Leave 2 tablespoons icing plain. Stir 2–3 teaspoons cocoa powder into yellow icing to make a caramel color. Combine remaining icing with remaining cocoa; blend until smooth. Spread caramel icing over entire cake.
4 Place dark-brown icing onto back and top of head. Use a fork to spread the brown and plain icing to other parts of the body. Decorate, as illustrated.

3. Cover the whole cake with caramel icing.

4. Spread brown icing with fork. Decorate with coconut and candy.

Rabbit Surprise

1 covered board
1 13 x 9 x 2-inch Basic
  Butter Cake
1 8-inch square Basic
  Butter Cake
1 quantity Fluffy Icing
black and pink food
  coloring
large pink or white
  marshmallows, cut in
  half, or miniature colored
  marshmallows
licorice strips
assorted candy

1. Shape cakes for head and hat.

2. Ice hat in black, rabbit head in pale grey.

1 Cut rectangular cake into rabbit head, as shown. Cut square cake into hat, as shown. (Note that rabbit is popping out of upside-down hat.) Assemble cakes on board. Divide icing in half. Tint one portion black; ⅓ cup pale pink, and remaining icing pale grey.
2 Spread black icing smoothly over hat. Swirl grey icing over head.
3 Pipe pink icing onto rabbit for ears and eyebrows, as shown.
4 Press marshmallows in straight rows onto hat. Decorate rabbit head with candy, as illustrated, using licorice strips for the whiskers, a pale pink jelly bean for the nose and a piece of red candy for the mouth.

3. Use pink icing for details on ears and face.

4. Decorate with marshmallows and candy.

HINT
Choosing candy for decorating is great fun, and tests your ingenuity. Popcorn and licorice makes good hair. Whites of eyes can be made with marshmallows, adding little colored candy-covered chocolate pieces for irises. You'll find it's easiest to use a sharp knife to cut sugar- and chocolate-coated candy. Licorice and marshmallows, lace, braid and ribbon are best cut with scissors.

1. Cut pound cake diagonally across whole length to make pitched roof.

2. Spread base with green icing, house with apricot, and roof with yellow.

Candy Cottage

1 covered board
1 13 x 9 x 2-inch Basic
    Butter Cake
2 frozen 7½ x 3-inch
    pound cakes, thawed
2 quantities Basic Butter
    Cream
yellow, apricot, green and
    violet food coloring
chocolate-covered graham
    crackers
small rectangular candy
colored sprinkles
assorted candy and cookies

1 Place rectangular cake onto prepared board. Position one of the pound cakes in the center of rectangular cake for the house. Cut the other pound cake diagonally across each side, the length of the pound cake, to form a pitched roof. Position onto house as roof. Secure with a little icing.

2 Divide icing into three portions. Reserve 1 tablespoon plain icing. Tint one portion yellow, one portion apricot and remainder green. Spread green icing over base, then apricot over house, followed by the yellow roof. Tint remaining yellow icing violet; use for curtains on windows.

3 Cut graham crackers in half diagonally. Position onto roof, as shown.

4 Make steps with bubble gum sticks or licorice twists; arrange rectangular candy around the front and sides of the cottage. Spread one cookie with reserved plain icing and decorate with sprinkles. This makes the front door. Use the other cookies for the windows. Don't forget the chimney. Decorate, as shown.

3. Cover roof with tiles made of graham crackers cut in half diagonally.

4. Trim with candy for steps, fence and front door, and finally the chimney.

Dreadful Dinosaur

1 covered board
2 8- or 9-inch round Basic
  Butter Cakes
1 quantity Basic Butter
  Cream
green and red food coloring
round milk chocolate
  mints, cut in half
green gumdrop leaves
candy for toes, eyes and
  brow

1 Cut one cake in half.
Cut two half circles
along flat side of each
cake half, as shown.
2 Cut second cake, as
shown in photograph.
3 Assemble cake on
prepared board, but do
not attach head. Tint all
but ⅓ cup icing green.
Tint 3 teaspoons icing
red; leave rest plain.
4 Spread green icing
over entire cake. Attach
head to body using

skewers; ice head. Use a
fork to spread plain icing
randomly over body.
Pipe red mouth onto
cake. Cut gumdrop
leaves down the center
and arrange along
dinosaur's head and
back. Press chocolate
mints over body at an
angle. Complete cake
with candy, as
illustrated.

HINT
For cake creature
mouths try candy
snakes, a red jelly
bean, or candy lips.
Black whiskers can be
made from licorice
strips and white
whiskers from
shredded coconut.
Finely cut licorice
makes good eyelashes
and brows.

1. Cut one cake in half, then cut out half
circles with cutter.

2. Cut second cake, as shown. This will
form the center body of the dinosaur.

3. *Assemble cake; ice body before attaching head with skewers then ice head.*

4. *Spread plain icing randomly over body. Finish dinosaur, as shown.*

Mr. Mouse

1 covered board
1 8- or 9-inch round Basic
   Butter Cake
1 quantity Basic Butter
   Cream
black, red and yellow food
   coloring
chocolate sprinkles
6 large round chocolate-
   covered cookies
1 large prune
1 large pink or white
   marshmallow
candy for eyes

1. Cut cake as shown; use cut-out piece for chin.

2. Ice face yellow; outline hair, cover with sprinkles.

1 Carefully cut into one side of cake to form nose, as shown. Place leftover cake under face to form Mr. Mouse's rounded chin. Assemble the cake in position on prepared board.
2 Tint ¼ cup icing black, ⅓ cup icing red, and make the remaining icing yellow. With a small metal spatula, spread yellow icing smoothly over entire face. Use a skewer to outline hair area. Fill area liberally with chocolate sprinkles, as shown.
3 Pipe outline of mouth onto cake with red icing, then fill in the area with red icing. Position three

3. Pipe and fill mouth. Outline features in black.

chocolate cookies on each side of head for each ear. Use black icing to outline eyes, brows and lashes, as well as nose.
4 Position prune on tip of the nose, fill in eyes with candy, and place marshmallow on cheek.

4. Add eyes, cookies for ears and prune for nose.

HINT
To make a cake of your child's favorite cartoon character, trace and then simplify it, keeping its identifying features. Use the colors associated with the character.

Casey Caterpillar

1 covered board
1 13 x 9 x 2-inch Basic
  Butter Cake
1 cupcake or muffin
1 quantity Fluffy Icing
apricot and green food
  coloring
jelly beans
assorted candy
plastic eyes
sugar lips
colored popcorn
8 inches of colored ribbon

1 Cut cake in half
lengthwise. Cut each
half of cake crosswise
into 6 pieces. Arrange
cake pieces on prepared
board as shown and
place cupcake at front
for head. Tint all but ¼
cup icing apricot; tint
reserved icing green.
2 Spread apricot icing
all over ends, top and
sides of line of cake and
over side of cupcake.

Spread top of cupcake
with green icing.
3 Press brightly colored
candy randomly onto
top, and pairs of jelly
beans at intervals along
sides of caterpillar as feet.
4 Decorate, as shown.

Note: Casey Caterpillar
is quick to assemble and
could easily be made by
children.

HINT
For a busy cook, you
can purchase pound
cakes or miniature
cream-filled cake rolls
for this recipe.
Simply cut the
pound cake into
twelve 3-inch pieces.
Then you can make
the icing or buy
canned ready-to-
spread icing
from the grocery
store.

1. Arrange cake pieces in wavy pattern on
board for body, with cupcake for head.

2. Cover ends, top and sides of body and
side of head with plain icing.

3. Press candy randomly over caterpillar body; ice top of head green.

4. Place eyes and lips in position; add popcorn hair, and finally the bow.

1. Place coconut and green food coloring in plastic bag and press between fingers.

2. Place cakes side-by-side on board and cover with green icing.

Soccer Field

1 covered board
2 13 x 9 x 2-inch Basic
    Butter Cakes
2 quantities Basic Butter
    Cream
green food coloring
½ cup flaked coconut
plastic soccer team with
    goal posts

1 Place cakes side-by-side on board. Place coconut in plastic bag with 2 drops food coloring. Press between fingers to mix. Tint all but ¼ cup icing pale green.
2 Ice cake green.
3 Place a 13 x 9 x 2-inch cake pan across center of field. Sprinkle coconut around pan. Remove pan.
4 Pipe field lines with plain icing. Position goal posts and players.

3. Sprinkle colored coconut around edges of the field.

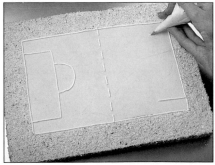

4. Pipe lines onto cake as shown, and position players and goal posts.

Tic-Tac-Toe

1 covered board
1 13 x 9 x 2-inch Basic
    Butter Cake
1 quantity Basic Butter
    Cream
pink and violet food
    coloring
licorice strips
frosted rectangular cookies
bubble gum sticks
candy-coated chocolate
    pieces
small piping bag

1 Place cake on
prepared board. Tint
all of icing deep pink
except for 1
tablespoon. Tint the
reserved icing violet.
Spread pink icing
smoothly over top of
the cake.
2 Press licorice strips
onto cake to make
squares, cutting as
necessary to fit.

3 Press chocolate-
coated candy pieces into
squares to make 'o's' and
use bubble gum sticks to
make the 'x's'. Cut these
to fit, as shown.
4 Ice back of cookies
and press around the
sides of cake. With violet
icing pipe 'you win' or
'happy birthday', or
whatever is appropriate.

HINT
There are all sorts of
other board games you
could make. For
instance, you could try
your hand at
backgammon, Chinese
checkers, or even
chess—use plastic
chess pieces, or as close
as you can get to them
using candy or cookies.
Your child may have a
particular favorite you
could make.

1. Frost top of cake with pink icing.

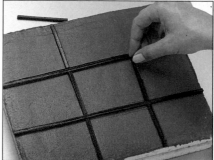

2. Press long thin strips of licorice onto cake
to form squares

3. Make 'o's' and 'x's' by pressing candy onto cake.

4. Press cookies around sides of cake as the finishing touch.

61

Kimberly Kite

1 covered board
2 13 x 9 x 2-inch Basic
   Butter Cakes
1 quantity Fluffy Icing
red food coloring
colored sprinkles
colored popcorn
2 chocolate-covered
   cookies
assorted candy
3 feet of curling ribbon

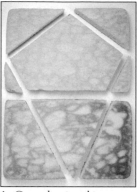

1. Cut cakes into kite shape, as shown.

2. Cover kite shape and triangles with white icing.

1 Arrange cakes side-by-side on a cutting surface. Cut cakes into shape of kite, as shown. Cut leftover cake into 2½-inch triangles. Position the kite and triangles onto the prepared board.
2 Tint ¼ cup icing red; leave remainder plain. Spread plain icing over top and sides of kite and triangles.
3 Decorate tops of triangles with sprinkles.
4 Pipe mouth onto cake with red icing, as shown. Decorate cake as illustrated with popcorn for hair, chocolate-covered cookies and candy for eyes, brows and nose, and curling ribbon for kite string. Finally, press cookies firmly around sides of kite.

3. Decorate triangles with colored sprinkles.

4. Pipe on mouth, add other facial features.

HINT

It's a lovely idea to make a cake that reflects your child's interests. You could make a baseball bat and ball, a football, a dart board, a book, or a basketball. More ambitious decorators could try a camera, a telephone or a computer. You could even try to make a portrait of your child, or show him or her engaged in some favorite activity. It doesn't have to be perfect—just be sure you get the eye and hair colors right.

Index